Maya Civilization

A History from Beginning to End

Copyright © 2020 by Hourly History.

All rights reserved.

Table of Contents

Introduction
Origins
The Preclassic Period: 2000 BCE-250 CE
Maya Religion and Medicine
The Classic Period: 250-900 CE
Maya Culture, Art, and Society
The Post-Classic Period: 900-1539 CE
Maya Weapons and Warfare
The Spanish Conquest: 1523-1697 CE
Maya Writing
Legacy of the Maya Civilization
Conclusion

Introduction

The Maya were one of the most important of the ancient peoples of Mesoamerica, dominating large areas of Central America and Mexico for more than one thousand years. They made important advances in writing, mathematics, medicine, and astronomy, and they built a whole series of cities featuring huge monumental architecture in rain forests and arid deserts.

We are still learning about the Maya and keep discovering and investigating the sites of their cities. Until relatively recently, it was believed that these people were mostly peaceful. We now know that they were the precise opposite and that war and warriors were an intrinsic part of most Maya societies. It was generally believed that the Maya followed the Olmec people and may have learned from them. The very latest thinking is that the Maya might have come before the Olmecs. We know that Maya culture rose then dramatically declined, but we have no idea why.

The one thing that most historians will agree on is that these were a people who were, in some ways, highly advanced. For example, scientists are now beginning to re-evaluate the Maya approach to health and medicine and are discovering that the holistic Maya view of these things fits very neatly with the latest theories about effective healing.

In other ways, the Maya never advanced much beyond the Stone Age during their long history. In terms of weapons and warfare, for example, the Maya retained the same ritualized approach throughout most of their ancient history. When they were confronted with invaders from medieval Europe, they were helpless to fight advanced weapons and tactics and were quickly conquered.

However, unlike many other cultures of Mesoamerica, the Maya survived, and Maya people, language, and culture survive to the present day in Mexico and Central America.

Chapter One

Origins

"The objects we were in search of were interesting, not only as the remains of an unknown people, but as works of art, proving, like newly discovered historical records, that the people who once occupied the Continent of America were not savages."

—John Lloyd Stephens

In the early to mid-1800s, few historians were interested in the ancient civilizations of the Americas. The people who had lived in these places were generally considered to have been primitive savages, and there had been no systematic attempt to carry out an archeological investigation of their sites. Then, in 1839, two travelers with an interest in history, American John Lloyd Stephens and Briton Frederick Catherwood, decided to travel to British Honduras (present-day Belize) to investigate mysterious ruins in the jungle.

Both men had been intrigued by accounts from earlier travelers to the area, including Jean-Frederic Maximilien, Comte de Waldeck, and Antonio del Rio. Deep in the uncharted jungles of Central America were ruins almost entirely obliterated by verdant growth. Stephens was a writer and Catherwood a talented artist, and together these men described in detail for the first time cities and monuments which had been forgotten even by the local people. These two men meticulously mapped, illustrated, and described the incredible sites they found, and what they discovered was instrumental in bringing to the attention of the world what would become known as the Maya civilization.

For the first time, it was realized that this ancient civilization was not a primitive society but a complex culture which had once dominated the area and created monuments and buildings which rivaled those created by other ancient civilizations elsewhere in the world.

The first humans to occupy the continents of North and South America are thought to have been groups of hunter-gatherers who arrived from Siberia towards the end of the Ice Age around 12,000 years ago. As these people spread south, they arrived in the area around the Gulf of Mexico somewhere around 9000-8000 BCE. The temperate climate and fertile land in this area led to a change in the way in which these people lived. From being nomadic hunters, they settled in small towns and villages and began to cultivate crops, which included maize, beans, tomatoes, avocado, and squash.

This area has become known to historians as Mesoamerica ("middle America"), and it includes parts of present-day Mexico and Costa Rica as well as the whole of Guatemala, Belize, El Salvador, Honduras, and Nicaragua. During the early period of the colonization of this area, there were no large urban centers, and most settled groups were small and lived in small villages near agricultural land and sources of water. As these people became more skilled in the cultivation of crops, they were able to produce food surpluses, which allowed populations to expand and even to begin the cultivation of luxury crops such as vanilla, chili, and cacao.

Having a reliable source of food enabled the creation of larger settlements and the development of more structured societies, which included ruling classes and specialists such as artisans who produced textiles as well as tools and weapons. By around 2000 BCE, this area entered what historians call the Preclassic Period, which saw an explosion of cultures that saw sudden advances in agriculture, science, and technology.

Chapter Two

The Preclassic Period: 2000 BCE-250 CE

"It is not good to look at the clouds or your work will not progress."

—Maya proverb

In the Preclassic Period, several civilizations emerged in Mesoamerica. The first and most significant were the mysterious Olmecs who appeared in the present-day Mexican states of Veracruz and Tabasco and at the Bay of Campeche on the Gulf Coast. No-one is entirely certain where the Olmecs came from—this culture seemed to arrive in Mesoamerica abruptly with its own developed religion, culture, language, science, and technology. There have been no discoveries of a gradual evolution or development of Olmec society, which has led to speculation these people may have arrived from outside the area. Some scholars suggest that the Olmecs may have come to the Americas from West Africa or ancient Egypt or that they may even have been Nordic incomers who had traveled from Europe. All that is certain is that these people established cities, art, architecture, and technology which gradually spread to many other parts of Mesoamerica.

The people who would become the Maya actually seem to have been in existence before the Olmecs. Settlements attributed to the Maya have been found in the Yucatán Peninsula which date back as far as 2600 BCE—no Olmec sites have been identified which are older than 1800 BCE. However, the earliest Maya sites are little more than large villages that show limited evidence of cultural or technological advance. When the Olmecs arrived, they brought with them science, particularly in terms of astronomical observation and the development of the calendar, as well as a form of writing and a religion which involved the first monumental architecture in Mesoamerica. The Olmecs also dominated trade in Mesoamerica and their ideas spread throughout the region. So, although the Maya existed before the Olmecs, it was the new technologies, arts, and sciences developed by the Olmecs that were borrowed by the Maya when they finally began to emerge as an important Mesoamerican culture.

The earliest Maya settlement identified by Archeologists is the village of Cuello in the humid lowlands in the north of present-day Belize. Up to the excavation of this site in 1975, it was believed that Maya civilization dated back to no more than 800 or 900 BCE and that the Maya followed after the Olmecs. However, though this site does include many buildings and artifacts from later phases of Maya culture, excavations also revealed the existence of much earlier settlements on the site that date back beyond 2000 BCE.

This is important because it confirms that the Maya was not a secondary culture which followed on from earlier civilizations but contemporaneous with the oldest

Mesoamerican cultures. Investigations at Cuello also tell us a little about the earliest Maya culture. There is evidence of trade with other Maya settlements—objects made from sandstone quarried 150 kilometers to the south and shells from the Caribbean coast 50 kilometers to the northeast have been recovered at this site.

Masks and other ornamental objects made from human skulls have also been found at this site, though we do not know whether these were relics of venerated ancestors or trophies from defeated enemies. The Maya villages of this period were small and comprised mainly thatched dwellings though there is also evidence that public shrines were created in larger villages. Tools during this period were primarily wood or stone and there was some creation of pottery. Food was still obtained through hunting, fishing, and gathering wild fruits and berries, but the farming of maize was becoming more common.

During the Middle Preclassic Period (1000-400 BCE) Maya settlements expanded and increased in number. There was increasing trade not just between Maya settlements but with other cultures such as the Olmecs. Maya society became increasingly complex with chiefs (who often claimed to be descended from the gods) controlling groups of settlements. The creation of a wealthy class generated demand for luxury items made from imported materials such as jade and obsidian. Agriculture became more advanced with developments in the creation of irrigation systems and canals and farms began to produce food surpluses which allowed the creation of an artisan class who began to create more sophisticated tools and weapons as well as artwork using carved stone and pottery. Large stone artworks were used to decorate public areas such as plazas in the largest settlements.

During the Late Preclassic Period (400 BCE-250 CE), Maya culture suddenly exploded. Maya scholars developed a system of mathematics, devised a calendar, and created a written language. Some Maya settlements, notably Kaminaljuyu and El Mirador, grew to become cities with large populations, public monuments and areas, pyramids, and ball courts, all decorated with carved scenes or painted murals. Major settlements were linked by paved roads which included bridges and causeways. Maya craftsmen began to produce fine ceramics and intricate jewelry. Trade became even more important, and major centers, such as Kaminaljuyu (on the site of present-day Guatemala City) which was associated with the trade in obsidian, grew in size and importance.

Inevitably, as populations grew there were also wars between chiefdoms to gain control of resources and land. Many Maya carvings from this period show leaders holding weapons and what appear to be captives taken during wars. Some cities, notably Kaminaljuyu, became the centers of powerful polities which dominated surrounding areas for decades or even longer.

However, towards the end of this period, in a phase which has become known as the Terminal Preclassic period, several important Maya cities were abandoned for reasons that are still not understood. Kaminaljuyu, for example, which had dominated the Guatemalan Highlands for hundreds of years and which had grown to include sophisticated irrigation systems and monumental architecture, was suddenly completely abandoned around

100 CE. No-one is certain why this happened. During this period, Maya settlements continued to increase in size and number, the Maya population continued to grow, and Maya cities generally became more sophisticated and their society more complex. Historians have speculated on possible causes and have suggested drought, volcanic eruption, invasion, deforestation, or some other unidentified agricultural failure, but all we can be certain about is that, towards the end of the Preclassic Period, the Maya abandoned several major cities, mainly in highland areas, and the population seems to have migrated towards lowland areas.

Abandonments of Maya settlements and cities peaked in the period 200-250 CE. This type of large-scale abandonment of important centers is often associated with the collapse of a culture, and yet that does not seem to have been the case here. The Maya continued to be a significant factor in the area, and the cities that they retained continued to grow and to become more powerful as these people moved towards the next phase of their culture.

Chapter Three
Maya Religion and Medicine

"The physical and spiritual worlds were at opposite ends of a continuum surrounded by medicine which aided the spirits in the healing process."

—Bonnie Bley

Maya religious beliefs are founded on the notion that everything on Earth, animate and inanimate, contains an element of the divine, *k'uh*. Everything on Earth was created by two deities, the Builder (*Tz'aqol*) and the Shaper (*B'itol*). The story of the creation of the Earth and everything in it is told in the *Popol Vuh* (Community Book). This was first written by a Maya scribe in the mid-sixteenth century, but it is based on a much older (and now lost) pictorial version.

The Community Book tells how the gods first made people out of mud, but these were not satisfactory because, although they could speak, they could not move or think. The gods destroyed the mud people and made a new race with the men being created out of wood and the women out of reeds. These were better, but they had no souls and did not respect the gods. These too were destroyed, and the gods created a third race of people, made from white and yellow maize dough mixed with the blood of the gods. These were real people, but they were so wise that they were perceived as a threat to the pantheon of gods. The supreme deity, Heart of Heaven, Huracán, intervened to cloud the eyes and minds of this new race to make them less wise. The gods were satisfied and this became the human race.

The Maya worshipped a bewildering array of gods. Confusingly, some could transform themselves into different gods and over time, some Maya gods seem to have changed in terms of their powers and abilities. In addition to the Builder, the Shaper, and Huracán, the principal Maya gods included:

Hun H'unahpu, the maize god. The god of life and fertility, generally portrayed as a young, handsome man with long hair.

K'inich Ajaw, the god of the sun. Respected and feared because, while sun is essential for agriculture and food, too much sun can cause drought and starvation. Often depicted as part or wholly a jaguar.

Chac, the rain god. Also respected and feared because rain was needed for agriculture but too much could cause flooding. Often depicted as part human, part reptile.

Kisim, the god of death and decay, often portrayed as a zombie-like creature of a skeleton.

Ix Chel, the goddess of rainbows. Rainbows in Maya culture were associated with bad luck—a Maya proverb noted, "Do not point at a rainbow or your finger will rot." This goddess is associated with disease and ill-luck.

The Maya believed that these deities and many more (more than one hundred fifty Maya gods have been identified) dwelt in the thirteen levels of the Upper World as well as in the nine levels of the Underworld with the Middle World (Earth) sited between. The Maya gods were worshipped through a number of rituals which included both bloodletting and sacrifice.

Bloodletting was confined to kings, queens, and members of royal families who were expected to provide some of their blood to be used in important rituals. These small quantities of blood were sometimes obtained in very painful ways using stingray spines or ropes with thorns embedded in them. In one ritual described in Maya writing, the queen was expected to pierce her tongue with a rope spiked with thorns to provide blood to sprinkle on important icons. Kings involved in the ritual were expected to do the same with their penis.

Many Maya rituals also involved human sacrifice. Generally, victims were prisoners of war though, if none were available, unfortunate Maya people might be selected to serve as sacrificial victims. Many sacrificial victims were killed by having their beating heart cut from their body; others were decapitated or simply thrown down deep natural wells. Many Maya religious rituals were carried out on pyramids which were built in religious complexes at the center of their cities. Maya pyramids were built with a flat area on top of which was a small temple, and it was in these temples that the most important rituals, including sacrifices, were carried out.

Not all Maya religious ritual involved the shedding of blood. For example, some rituals were complex dances with the participants wearing elaborate costumes depicting gods. Other rituals involved giving precious objects to the gods, and even certain ball games formed part of important religious rituals. Some specific rituals involved lowering young children on ropes into deep natural wells. After several hours, the child would be brought back to the surface and asked whether they had received any messages from the gods. Marriages were also a source of complex religious rituals though divorce was also acceptable to the Maya if a marriage did not produce children.

The Maya also believed that each person had an animal spiritual companion (*Way' ob*) which shared their soul. They believed that, in certain circumstances, a person could transform into their Way' ob. Kings and other royal personages were associated specifically with the jaguar, but ordinary people could share their soul with almost any type of animal. Certain senior priests were thought to have more than one Way' ob and were capable of transforming into several different animals.

Maya priests were amongst the first systematic astronomers, and this helped them to develop a calendar (some historians believe this was derived from ideas first developed by the Olmecs) and a system of mathematics which included the use of zero as a number. These Maya astronomers were amazingly accurate in their observations—they calculated that the average lunar month lasted 29.5308 days. Modern scientists using computers have calculated the actual length of the average lunar month as 29.53059 days.

There was also a strong connection for the Maya between religion and health. The Maya believed in *ch'ulel* (life-force) in the body. Illness was seen as caused by an imbalance in the ch'ulel which was caused by both physical and spiritual factors. Healers (*h'men*) used a combination of treatments derived from plants, herbs, and acupuncture with religious ritual designed to rebalance the ill person's ch'ulel. This holistic view that illness is neither wholly physical or spiritual but a combination of both is something that many other ancient cultures believed and is followed by many people today as it has become accepted that physical and emotional health are linked.

Chapter Four

The Classic Period: 250-900 CE

"It is not good to hide good food from visitors because it will turn into worms."

—Maya proverb

During the Classic Period, Maya culture and influence reached their zenith. There were up to two million Mayans, most living in cities which ranged in size from ten thousand to over fifty thousand occupants. Cities became powerful city-states, often extending their power and influence to surrounding areas. Maya society became increasingly urbanized, stratified, and complex, and Maya engineers and scientists made important advances in agriculture, construction, astronomy, cosmology, and writing. The Classic Period is generally divided into two phases: The Early Classic (250-600 CE) and the Late Classic (600-900 CE).

The beginning of the Classic Period is marked by the first appearance of dated stone monuments. These dates are based on a 365-day year and an origin date of 3114 BCE. These include altars, stelae (tall, carved stone shafts), and carved stone blocks. These tell the story of Maya culture through the recording of important social, religious, military, and political events, and it is through these that historians have been able to piece together the story of the development of Maya culture and the spread of Maya civilization.

During the Classic Period, there were up to forty cities with populations ranging from five to fifty thousand. The largest and most powerful included Tikal, Uaxactún, Copán, Bonampak, Dos Pilas, Calakmul, Palenque, and Río Bec. Each city was ruled by a king known as a *kuhul ajaw* (holy lord), who was regarded as a semi-divine being able to mediate between ordinary people and the gods. Kingship was hereditary, and the participation of kings and members of the royal families was an important element of many religious rituals.

Many Maya cities of the Classic Period were located in the southern lowlands in areas of rainforest. This was in contrast to the Olmecs who had gone before and other contemporary cultures such as that based in the city of Teotihuacan which were located in highland areas where irrigation and the conservation of limited water supplies were much more important. The Maya had access to diverse natural resources including limestone (used for construction) and obsidian which was used in the manufacture of tools and weapons.

During the Early Classic Period, the development of Maya civilization and culture was influenced by the city of Teotihuacan in present-day Mexico. This was not a Maya city, but it was the largest and most powerful city in Mesoamerica during this period. The city of Teotihuacan covered over eight square miles and had a population of more than one hundred thousand people. There was a great deal of trade between Teotihuacan and Maya cities, including the city of Tikal in present-day Guatemala. Tikal had become dominant politically and militarily in the Maya heartlands, and its king, Chak Tok Ich'aak (Great Jaguar Paw), was one of the most powerful of all the Maya leaders.

Then, in 378 CE, the rulers of Teotihuacan seem to have decided that the city of Tikal was becoming a threat. We don't know precisely what caused this, but the city of Teotihuacan sent an army under the command of a notable military leader, Siyaj K'ak' (Born of Fire), marching south to attack Tikal. After a brief battle, the Maya forces defending Tikal were defeated and its king was killed. Soon after, Siyaj K'ak' installed a new king in Tikal, Yax Nuun Ahiin (First Crocodile), who was the son of one of the lords of Teotihuacan. Under the rue of this new dynasty, Tikal became one of the two most important Maya cities.

The city grew to cover more than six square miles and incorporated more than three thousand permanent structures. Tikal is located in present-day Guatemala, in an area of verdant rainforest and fertile soil. The city was located on a junction of the major east-west trade route across the Yucatán Peninsula, making it an important stop for travelers and merchants. The city was dominated by a temple complex at its center which included a huge, stepped pyramid over 150 feet tall.

With the support of Teotihuacan, Tikal quickly became the most important Maya city in the area, directly controlling the lands which surrounded the city. Many smaller Maya cities in the Petén Basin including Uaxactun and Bejucal became vassal cities, and a system of ditches and defensive ramparts were built to protect Tikal from attack. At its peak, it is believed that the city of Tikal was the home to more than 100,000 people.

Yet Tikal was not the only significant Maya city during the Classic period. One hundred miles to the northwest of Tikal was another Maya city that would become its main rival—Calakmul. This city, located in the northern Petén Basin region of the Yucatán Peninsula in present-day Mexico, was the center of what has become known as the Kingdom of the Snake. Like Tikal, Calakmul came to dominate the other Maya cities in the surrounding area, and by the Classic Period, its population had grown to over 50,000 people. Also like Tikal, the center of this city was dominated by a temple complex which incorporated a tall stepped pyramid.

The Classic Period of the Maya civilization was dominated by the rivalry between Tikal and Calakmul as each strove to become the main city of the Maya. Partly, this was a struggle for control of natural resources and trade, but it also seems to have been based on ideological differences. Tikal, dominated by a dynasty transplanted from Teotihuacan in the north, placed great emphasis on the single male ruler of the city. In Calakmul, there was more emphasis on the role of the female line, and the king and queen seem to have been regarded as a ruling partnership.

Whatever the causes of the conflict, the struggle for supremacy of these two cities dominated the Classic Period. For a time, Calakmul seemed to be succeeding by carefully building a series of alliances with smaller city-states which resulted in Tikal being completely surrounded by hostile areas. Then, in 695 CE, the armies of Tikal and Calakmul finally faced one another in open battle. The outcome was a decisive victory for Tikal, and within 50 years, Tikal was able to defeat most of Calakmul's allies and to dismantle the city's system of alliances. By the Late Classic Period, Tikal had once again become the pre-eminent Maya city.

Yet neither Tikal nor Calakmul were to survive the mysterious events which have become known as the Late Classic Maya Collapse. By around 900 CE, the once-thriving and powerful city of Tikal had been abandoned to the jungle. Calakmul had descended into chaos with no one central ruler, and that city too entered a period of decline and abandonment.

Historians still debate what caused the decline of these cities. There was certainly continuing warfare between Tikal and Calakmul as well as other Maya cities, including Copán and Quiriguá. It has been speculated that this caused the population to concentrate in urban areas and that this in turn led to over-farming in areas close to cities, deforestation, and eventually to an ecological collapse which meant that cities such as Tikal and Calakmul were not able to produce enough food to feed their populations.

It has also been suggested that there may have been an invasion from the outside by a non-Maya people. There is certainly some evidence that, for example, the Toltec people from the Gulf Coast lowlands may have occupied some former Maya territory, but it is not certain whether this happened after the Maya cities had already been weakened by other causes. A long-lasting drought has also been suggested as the cause of the abandonment of Maya cities, as has a sudden spread of some infectious disease or some disruption to the trade upon which the Maya cities had come to depend.

None of these theories are universally accepted, and the reason for the decline of once-powerful Maya cities towards the end of the ninth century CE remains one of the great archeological mysteries. All we can be certain about is that Maya cities such as Tikal were thriving metropolises in around 800 CE, capable of exerting considerable influence on the surrounding area. Little more than 100 years later, these cities were abandoned ruins rapidly being reclaimed by the jungle. But although the end of the Classic Period brought the abandonment of some important Maya cities, it did not mean the end for the Maya civilization.

Chapter Five

Maya Culture, Art, and Society

"The greatest wisdom is in simplicity. Love, respect, tolerance, sharing, gratitude, forgiveness. It's not complex or elaborate. The real knowledge is free."

—Carlos Barrios, Maya elder and Ajq'ij of the Eagle Clan

During the Classic Period, most Maya polities were small city-states (*ajawil*) ruled by a hereditary king (*k'uhul ajaw*). In that sense, there wasn't a single overall Maya society but rather a series of separate small states, each with their own ruling group but which shared a language and certain cultural values.

Most of these polities were small, generally consisting of no more than a single central city and a series of nearby towns ruled by that city. There were exceptions—Tikal and Caracol, for example, ruled more extensive areas, but during the Classic Period, the lands controlled by the Maya comprised a patchwork of small cities and dependent towns, each competing with others for control of natural resources and trade routes.

Within each polity, the central group was the royal family. Cities were typically constructed so that palaces occupied by members of this family and temples formed the center of the city and contained all its important public spaces. Nobles and those responsible for the administration of the city-state also lived in large residences close to the center of the city while poorer families lived in small, often temporary housing on the periphery of the city or even outside its defensive walls.

Below the royal family were the nobles, those members of high-status families who served as military leaders, important priests, and government officials. Most nobles were literate and well-educated, and most noble families were very wealthy. Next in rank below the nobles were the commoners, the mass of ordinary Maya people. These ranged from servants and laborers to artisans and wealthy merchants. In general, commoners were not able to become nobles though there is evidence in some Maya societies that it was possible for a commoner who served valiantly in the military to be promoted to noble status.

Slavery was common amongst the Maya. Unwanted children could become slaves as could prisoners captured during war, and any member of Maya society could be sold into slavery if times were hard. In some cases, slavery was used as a punishment for certain crimes including failure to pay debts. The child of a slave would not automatically become a slave, but a man or woman who chose to marry a slave would also become a slave. The royal family, nobles, and commoners were all permitted to own slaves. If a slave's owner died, the slave would generally be sacrificed so that they could continue to serve their master after death.

The ancient Maya practiced several forms of body modification, often as a means of differentiating between social classes. One of the most notable examples was the cranial modification practiced on members of the royal family. The skulls of very young babies were tightly bound while they were still soft resulting in a skull elongated towards the rear or vertically. It is thought that the Maya may have adopted this practice from the Olmecs. This resulted in a long thin skull shape which echoed the head shape used in sculptures and images of Maya gods, emphasizing the link between divinely chosen members of the royal family and the gods themselves. There is some evidence that cranial modification became more widespread in the later years of Maya culture perhaps as nobles tried to make their children look more like those of the king and royal family.

Being cross-eyed (known in medical terms as the condition strabismus) was also seen as evidence of a connection to the gods. Many royal children were trained to become cross-eyed by dangling beads or other colorful objects very close to their eyes from an early age. If this was done regularly, it could produce a permanent cross-eyed condition which was regarded as a sign of extremely high status.

The ancient Maya also practiced elaborate modification of their teeth. From the Early Preclassic Period on, many Maya had their teeth filed into geometric shapes or points. Warriors in particular often had their teeth filed into sharp points to resemble the teeth of a predatory animal but women, particularly women of high status, also had their teeth filed into different shapes. In addition to filing, many Maya remains show evidence of having holes drilled in front teeth and these then being filled with inlays made from precious stones or other materials such as jade or turquoise. These dental modifications were much more common amongst the Maya than the cranial modification which was mainly confined to the royal family and nobles.

Piercings and tattoos were also very common amongst the ancient Maya of all classes. Ears, lips, cheeks, and noses were pierced at a very early age, and increasing sizes of inserts made from precious stones or other colorful stones were inserted as the child grew. Tattoos were used both as body decoration and as punishment for certain crimes—a convicted thief, for example, might be punished by having his face tattooed in a certain way.

Maya also used colorful body painting to make themselves even more noticeable. The color red was often used, sometimes on the face and sometimes the whole body and generally by high-status members of society during important ceremonies. Sacrificial victims in religious ceremonies were also sometimes painted; it seems that blue was commonly used in these circumstances.

Clothes worn by all classes of Maya were colorful and made from fabrics derived from cotton, hemp, and other fibers. Fibers were dyed into bright colors and then woven into complex geometrical designs. Nobles and members of the royal family wore hats which were extremely large and elaborate. These hats were sometimes decorated with feathers, something that was permitted only high-status members of society—commoners were not allowed to decorate their clothing with feathers.

Maya art took several forms. In addition to the ceramic items used in day-to-day life, Maya artisans produced delicately painted and carved decorative pottery. Mainly produced without the use of a wheel, this pottery showed scenes from Maya mythology as well as important social events and even texts taken from important works. These objects were clearly very precious to high-status Maya and were often buried with their owners. These ceramic items are not only beautiful, but they have also provided archeologists with important clues as to Maya life and society.

Many Maya public buildings and spaces from the Classic Period on featured stone sculptures, often depicting deities, rulers, and scenes from Maya history and mythology. Interior spaces in residences and public spaces were often adorned with colorful painted murals, sometimes showing mythological or historical scenes but often depicting aspects of everyday life. Sadly, the humidity in Central America and Mexico means that relatively few of these murals have survived, but those that have show that Maya artists were capable of producing beautiful and engaging artwork. It is also thought that carved wood was used by many Maya artists and artisans but, for the same reason, very little has survived.

With the throngs of people with tattoos, painted faces, piercings, and modified teeth and colorful murals and ceramics, ancient Maya cities must have been eye-catching and vibrant places.

Chapter Six

The Post-Classic Period: 900-1539 CE

"For the Maya, the Post-Classic period was a time of complex and profound changes."

—Sylvanus Griswold Morley, *The Ancient Maya*

Although the end of the Classic Period saw the abandonment of some major Maya cities in the southern lowlands, Maya civilization did not disappear. Instead, the Maya concentrated in the northern Yucatán Peninsula. Maya cities already in the area grew, and new cities were built. The Maya in the Post-Classic Period, however, faced some new challenges. One of the most notable was the switch from cities located mainly in a damp, humid, rainforest environment to the much drier climate of the Yucatán Peninsula.

The city which came to dominate this period in Maya history was Chichén Itzá, in northern Yucatán. This city had been founded around 600 CE, but it wasn't until the abandonment of Tikal and Calakmul in 900 CE that it became the largest and most prosperous Maya city. As Chichén Itzá became more prominent, two other Maya cities in the immediate area—Yaxuna in the south and Coba in the east—began to diminish in size and importance. These two cities had previously been allies, but as first Coba and then Yaxuna lost territory to Chichén Itzá, both became notably less powerful.

    Thus, during the tenth century, Chichén Itzá became the most important cultural, military, political, and trade center of the Maya civilization. The central part of the city—comprising temples and residences for the king, the royal family, and important nobles—covered more than five square kilometers. The temples in the center of the city were built on an area which was artificially leveled and included the Temple of Xtoloc and the Temple of Kukulcan, which incorporated a stepped pyramid over 100 feet tall. This pyramid, *El Castillo*, is more than simply a monument to Maya religion—it is the Maya calendar set in stone. Each of the four staircases has 91 steps and when added together with the single step leading to the main temple gives a total of 365 steps. Precisely at sunset on the spring equinox, the heads and tails of the serpents which decorate the main staircase are joined by a body of shadow. The orientation and placement of decoration on this pyramid also highlight many other important events within the Maya calendar. To create such a precisely aligned stone building of this size would be challenging in any circumstances, but to do so without the benefit of the wheel or metal tools and solely using human muscle is an astonishing achievement.

    The central part of Chichén Itzá also incorporated more than 13 ball courts—the games played in these courts were not simply sport but formed part of religious rituals. The largest ball court, the Great Ball Court, is the largest ever discovered in the Americas, measuring over 550 feet in length and incorporating the Temple of the Jaguar built into one of its walls. This central part of the city was surrounded by a much larger expanse of smaller and sometimes temporary residences.

All the important buildings in the central part of Chichén Itzá were linked by raised, paved causeways called *sacbeob*, which linked the various parts of the city and extended out into the surrounding countryside. Excavations show that the buildings in the central part of the city were originally painted in bright colors, mainly red, green, blue, and purple, and this part of the city must have been a vibrant and colorful place in its heyday.

The city of Chichén Itzá became not just the largest Maya city but also one of the most important trade centers in the Yucatán Peninsula. The city established a port at nearby Isla Cerritos on the north coast of the Yucatán, and trade through this post included gold from southern Central America and obsidian from Mexico. By 1050 CE, Chichén Itzá controlled most of northern and central Yucatán and had become the new center of Maya culture.

Although this was the largest of the Post-Classic Maya cities, it wasn't the only one; Mayapán, sixty miles west of Chichén Itzá, and Uxmal, ninety miles south-west, both became important cities during the Post-Classic Period. Like Chichén Itzá, both these cities featured centers that incorporated many temple complexes and stepped pyramids, and each also had a network of *sacbeob* which crisscrossed the Yucatán and became the main trade routes within the region.

All the Maya cities in this period faced a particular problem: shortage of water. The Yucatán is generally dry and arid, especially compared to the rain forest locations of many of the Classic Period Maya cities. Most of the water in the Yucatán is retained in natural underground reservoirs, and all these cities incorporated sacred wells which tapped into this supply of water. It is no coincidence that, while the frequency of Maya religious ritual seems to have decreased during this period, worship of Chac, the Maya rain god, increased.

Chichén Itzá continued to dominate the Yucatán until around 1250 CE when it began to decline in importance and size. No-one is quite certain why, though some accounts suggest that the city may have been sacked by troops from Mayapán. It is certainly true that, during the period when Chichén Itzá was in decline, Mayapán became more powerful until, by 1300, it was the most significant of all the Maya cities, and it is from this city that the name of the civilization is taken.

During the Post-Classic Period, Maya influence was no longer the only cultural contribution to life in the Yucatán. When the once-mighty city of Teotihuacan collapsed, a new culture arose in present-day Mexico—the Toltecs. These people spread their beliefs across Mexico and Central America, and Maya cities including Chichén Itzá, Mayapán, and Uxmal all display clear signs of the assimilation of Toltec culture. For example, carvings in all three cities represent Quetzalcoatl, the Toltec feathered serpent, the Toltec rain god Tlaloc, and the Toltec Jaguar cult emblem. Historians are not certain what the precise relationship was between the Maya and the Toltecs, but it is clear that there was an extensive exchange of ideas between these two cultures.

During the Post-Classic Period, maritime trade became increasingly important to the Maya who traded with many partners in Central America. However, the period from 1250 onwards is generally one of gradual decline for the Maya. There was less building of large monumental structures, and many Maya cities grew smaller. At around the same time, the Toltec capital at Tula was destroyed during a war, and the Toltec Empire collapsed entirely.

There have been many attempts to explain the decline of the Maya and their neighbors including suggestions that environmental changes may have led to a reduction in levels of agricultural produce, but it seems likely that the gradual decline of the Maya cities was also made worse by the almost continual state of warfare which existed between Maya city-states. The Maya were clearly a warlike people, and wars, both large and small, seem to have been an inherent part of the Maya world. Many Maya sculptures and carvings of the Post-Classic Period are concerned with images of conflict and violence.

These continuing wars combined with living in the arid Yucatán all seem to have contributed to the decline of the Maya. Then, in the late 1400s, the first Spanish ships appeared off the coast of Central America.

Chapter Seven

Maya Weapons and Warfare

"Conflict is seen as central to Maya society throughout its history."

—David Webster, The Not So Peaceful Civilization: A Review of Maya War

War was a recurring feature of the Maya way of life. In the Pre-Classic and Early Classic Periods, wars between rival city-states were undertaken in order to take control of trade routes, to assure sources of food and resources, and to take captives who could be used as slaves or even as sacrifices during religious rituals. In the Late Classic and Post-Classic Periods, increasing populations combined with a drop in agricultural output due to drought and other environmental factors provided even more reasons for conflict. Maya cities founded during these later periods were not placed close to productive land but sited in easily defended locations and often incorporated large defensive walls and other structures.

War and the taking and sacrifice of prisoners are often depicted in Maya artworks, which makes it odd that until around 50 years ago, the Maya were considered to be a very peaceful society that rarely became involved in wars.

It wasn't until the decipherment of Maya hieroglyphs that historians learned the full extent of Maya warfare. It is now generally accepted that the city-states which comprised the Maya culture were often at war with one another as well as with outsiders. These wars ranged in size from small raids on neighboring villages in order to plunder and obtain prisoners to full-scale invasions of another territory for the purpose of incorporating it into the land of the attacker.

Information about the organization and deployment of Maya armies is scarce. It is assumed that each Maya city-state had its own army, but it is not known whether this was a conscript army where citizens were called up only when they were needed to fight or a professional standing army such as that used by the Aztecs. The most popular theory is that members of the noble class became professional warriors and that these men passed on their knowledge to their sons, resulting in a hereditary warrior class within Maya society, though it is likely that the numbers of these warriors were very small. It appears that the king of each city-state had control of the army of that city and it is thought that the armies themselves were most likely fairly small—probably no more than 1,000 men in total for large campaigns and far fewer for small raids.

Most Maya military weapons and equipment were light and easily transported. Maya city-states were anything up to 50 kilometers apart, and traveling between cities meant crossing rain forests and other difficult terrains so all military gear had to easily transportable by individual soldiers.

Maya weapons can be divided into two classes: ranged weapons and melee weapons. Ranged weapons included the *hulche*, a development of the *atlatl* first seen in Teotihuacan. This was a shaft with a cup on one end which was used to throw a light, obsidian tipped spear a considerable distance. In the Post-Classic Period, Maya armies also began to use the bow and arrow. Perhaps the most surprising Maya ranged weapon was the hornet bomb—some Maya accounts describe how a hornet's nest would be located and then sealed within a light clay shell. This would be launched into enemy lines, and as it fell, the clay shell would break, releasing clouds of maddened hornets into enemy lines.

After ranged weapons had been discharged, Maya armies would then engage in melee combat. For this they used heavier spears as well as axes, clubs, and maces, often incorporating obsidian blades or tips. Many Maya warriors carried shields made from wood and covered in thick, knotted rope. Soldiers did not wear anything resembling armor, though some depictions seem to show heavy infantry wearing some protective clothing made from palm fibers.

What little we know about Maya warfare suggests that this was heavily ritualized. Before any combat, warriors would take part in dances and other rituals, and the clothing warriors wore is often depicted as resembling the clothing of priests, with elaborate head-dresses and masks and ornamentation which recalls Maya deities. Warriors became revered members of society depending on their performance in battle and especially their ability to kill or capture enemies of high rank.

War and weapons are often depicted in Maya artwork of all kinds, and the practice and ritual of war was clearly important to these people. When this first became apparent in the 1960s, it surprised some historians who had until that time considered the Maya to be largely peaceful. This led to a theory that increasing violence and war led to the collapse of Maya society at the end of the Classic Period, though this too has been largely discredited by more recent discoveries. War became even more common in the Late Classic and Post-Classic Periods, yet this does not seem to have been the direct cause of the Maya decline but rather a response to the increasing scarcity of food and resources. War was important to the Maya, but its practice seems to have been confined to a relatively small warrior elite, and war alone did not bring about the collapse and abandonment of Maya cities.

Chapter Eight

The Spanish Conquest: 1523-1697 CE

"We came here to serve God and the King, and also to get rich."

—Bernal Díaz del Castillo

In 1492, Christopher Columbus discovered the New World on behalf of the Spanish Kingdom of Castile and Leon. Soon after, Spanish adventurers began to colonize the Caribbean and established a regional capital on the island of Cuba. Gradually, the Spanish brought more troops and weapons to the area until, by 1521, they were able to conquer the Aztec capital city of Tenochtitlan in present-day Mexico. Within a few years, Spanish control of the area expended to cover most of Mexico as far south as the Isthmus of Tehuantepec. The Spanish Crown then formally established the Viceroyalty of New Spain in 1535, which meant that all Spanish-held land in America belonged to the Spanish king.

One of the first attempts by Spanish explorers to investigate Maya lands was the voyage undertaken in 1517 by Francisco Hernández de Córdoba. Hernández sailed with a small fleet from Cuba to explore the coastline of the Yucatán Peninsula. After a number of adventures, the small

Spanish group was attacked by a large group of Maya warriors while they were ashore seeking fresh water. Many were killed, and Hernández was seriously wounded. The small fleet was able to return to Cuba where Hernández died soon after, but not before describing the gold he had found while exploring Maya cities on the Yucatán.

In 1519, a fleet of 11 Spanish ships carrying over 500 men under the command of Hernán Cortés returned to the Yucatán to search for Maya gold. The fleet anchored at Potonchán, a Chontal Maya town and the capital of the Maya city-state of Tabasco. The Maya attacked, but the Spanish troops—some mounted, most wearing armor, and many equipped with firearms—easily defeated the Maya warriors. The defeated Maya then provided Cortés with food and gold.

When the Aztec city of Tenochtitlan fell to the Spanish in 1521, many Maya became concerned, and several Maya city-states attempted to make peace with Cortés and his men. Despite this, in 1523, Cortés sent one of his lieutenants, Pedro de Alvarado, with 180 cavalry, 300 infantry, and 4 cannons to attack the Maya in present-day Guatemala. The campaign in Guatemala was to last six years and, by 1530, the Spanish were in almost complete control of the lands formally ruled by the Maya.

Part of the reason was the superiority of Spanish military equipment, weapons, and tactics—against these, the primitive weapons and ritualized combat of the Maya proved to be almost completely ineffective. In addition, there was another factor in the ease with which the Spanish overcame much larger numbers of indigenous people. When they arrived, the Spanish brought with them diseases from Europe to which the Maya had no resistance. Much like what would happen to the Native American Indian tribes in North America, epidemics of infectious diseases such as smallpox devastated the Maya population in Guatemala.

In 1526, Francisco de Montejo was granted permission by the Spanish Crown to colonize the Yucatán Peninsula. In December of that year, Montejo left Spain with four ships and four hundred men. Once again, Spanish military technology proved unstoppable, and by 1535, the Spanish controlled virtually all of the Yucatán. The only other Maya stronghold located in the Chiapas Highlands was conquered by another Spanish nobleman, Pedro de Portocarrero, by 1547.

There was an uprising by the Maya in the Yucatán in 1545, but this was easily crushed by the Spanish. Under Spanish control, the Maya people became a source of cheap labor, relocated and forced to work where necessary to ensure the continuing supply of riches to Spain. Disease and other hardships took their toll, and Maya populations fell in all areas. The Spanish conquerors introduced Christianity to the area as well as European methods of agriculture and manufacturing, changing the nature of society for the surviving Maya. Still, Maya culture and society did not disappear after the Spanish conquest. Instead, many Maya fled to sparsely populated areas such as the Western Petén Basin in order to avoid contact with the Spanish.

Chapter Nine

Maya Writing

"Finally, there is still hope that . . . there is still a place somewhere in the Mayab where a large number of ancient books are kept. Well-hidden and preserved at best, they wait there for the discovery by a lucky archaeologist."

—Christian Schoen

One of the most notable aspects of the Maya was their development of a hieroglyphic script. This written language was much more complex and sophisticated than earlier written languages developed by, for example, the Olmecs. Maya writing used both pictograms, symbols which represent objects and actions, with ideograms, which represent more abstract things like ideas or symbolic actions, and phonetic glyphs, which represent sounds. Earlier written languages had used only pictograms, but the language developed by the Maya allowed the expression and recording of much more complex writing.

Some historians have suggested that Maya writing was the only complete writing system in Mesoamerica. Originally, it was believed that Maya writing may have been developed from earlier written languages such as Olmec, but discoveries made in 2005 suggest that Maya writing may actually pre-date Olmec, and it may be that the

Maya were the first people to invent writing in Mesoamerica.

Maya writing seems to have first emerged in the Middle Pre-Classic Period, around 300 BCE. By the Early Classic Period, around 250 CE, Maya writing seems to have been fully developed and changed little throughout the remainder of Maya civilization. Most of the surviving Maya script comes from carved stone monuments and recovered ceramic artifacts. From approximately the ninth century CE, most Maya writing was done on paper made from bark or on dried deerskin. This was used to create books but, partly due to the damp, humid climate and partly due to destruction caused during the Spanish occupation, very few of these have survived. The Spanish viewed Maya writings as potentially subversive, and many were deliberately destroyed—when Bishop Diego de Landa arrived in the Yucatán in 1549, for example, one of his first acts was to order the burning of all Maya writings. Only a handful of Maya writing on paper or deerskin remain, and all are held in museums in Europe or Mexico.

Over time, Maya script used around 1,000 different symbols, though at any one time, only around 500 were in use. These symbols were arranged in blocks and displayed in double columns. Text is read starting from the top left and moving horizontally to the end of the second column and then moving to the block below.

Writing was seen as sacred to the Maya. The god Itzamna was said to have invented writing, and two gods, Hun Batz and Hun Chuen, were often represented as the scribes of the gods. The ability to read and write is not thought to have been widespread amongst the Maya—

probably only priests, nobles, and royal personages were literate, though it is notable that both men and women seem to have been taught.

The Maya system of writing influenced later Mesoamerican writing systems such as that developed by the Aztec. After the Spanish occupation of the Maya lands, Maya writing was suppressed as being pagan and un-Christian. Although it seems that many Maya continued to write as late as the eighteenth century, this was done in secret, and by the twentieth century, knowledge of Maya writing had disappeared almost completely.

It wasn't until the 1950s that the Soviet linguist Yuri Knorozov began the task of deciphering Maya script. The earliest attempts to translate Maya script assumed that each symbol equated to a letter. Knorozov was one of the first scholars to suggest that some of the symbols in Maya script represented objects while some others were sounds. This understanding expanded until, at the current time, the vast majority of Maya symbols and glyphs are understood and the writings of the ancient Maya are accessible.

Chapter Ten

Legacy of the Maya Civilization

"We are not myths of the past, ruins in the jungle or zoos. We are people and we want to be respected, not to be victims of intolerance and racism."

—Rigoberta Menchú Tum

The Maya people were not destroyed by the Spanish occupation, and today there are many thriving communities of Maya in Mexico, Honduras, El Salvador, Belize, and Guatemala. There are large Maya groups in Mexico with the largest being the Yucatecs from the Yucatán, who number around 300,000, and the Tzotzil and Tzeltal from the Chiapas Highlands, who number around 200,000. Guatemala is still considered the birthplace of the Maya civilization, and the population of that country includes 60% who come from Maya ethnic groups. It has been estimated that there are as many as eight million Maya living in America.

Some have become integrated into modern urban life but some, in spite of the Spanish occupation and the incursion of other people into their lands, have succeeded in maintaining their cultural identity and continuing a recognizably Maya way of life. A few groups in remote areas such as the Lacandón in the Chiapas rain forest were never Christianized and continue to practice a version of the ancient Maya religion.

Modern land management and agricultural practices, as well as intensive industries such as logging, have threatened the Maya way of life in many areas, but this is now recognized in some countries and there are efforts underway to preserve the Maya. In Guatemala, for example, around 40% of the Petén Basin has been designated as the Maya Biosphere Reserve, and in 1985, an article was added to the Guatemalan constitution recognizing the Maya people and respecting their right to speak their own languages and practice their own culture.

As more is understood about the ancient Maya and the importance of this culture is appreciated, there is increasing interest in preserving the cultural heritage of these people and the sites and artifacts that they left behind. Although Spanish is the official language of most of Central America, the Maya language is now taught in some schools. In total, more than 20 dialects spoken by people in Central America can be traced back directly to ancient Mayan.

Modern scientists have even begun to re-examine in detail some of the herbal and plant-based healing used by the ancient Maya. Some of these have proven to be surprisingly effective, and other modern research also seems to support the overall concept of illness first suggested by the Maya. The ancient Maya understood illness as a symptom of imbalance between the body and the soul—imbalance meant illness, while balance meant good health. This connects neatly with recent attempts to find a more holistic way of dealing with illness rather than simply treating symptoms with drugs.

The legacy of the Maya extends well beyond ruins in the jungle and artifacts in museums. Unlike most ancient cultures, the Maya still exist, and their customs and culture are increasingly becoming seen as worthy of preservation and study.

Conclusion

Unlike many ancient people, the Maya were not a single, homogenous group. Although they originated in a common area, these people rapidly spread across Central America and Mexico and formed their own separate city-states. Each city may have worshipped the same gods and most spoke and wrote a dialect based on the same language, but each was also recognizably different and had its own culture, society, and governance.

This fragmentation into a host of small city-states led to diversity in language, culture, art, and even in the formation and structure of different Maya societies. It also meant that there existed an almost continual state of competition between disparate Maya groups. No one group became sufficiently powerful to dominate the others, and the resulting almost continual state of warfare weakened the Maya overall.

The Maya made startling advances in some areas—the development of writing, mathematics, medicine, and astronomy, for example—but in other areas, they remained virtually unchanged for their whole history. The Maya never developed metalworking or the wheel. While in some respects their culture and society were highly advanced, in other ways the Maya remained in the Stone Age.

When the Spanish arrived in America, the fragmented tribes of the Maya, like all the other Mesoamerican cultures, were powerless to resist attackers armed with modern weapons and armor and using effective rather than ritualized military tactics. However, unlike some other cultures, the Maya survived the Spanish occupation, and Maya language, society, and ideas survive to the present day.

We are still learning about these ancient people, but it is certain that the Maya were one of the most important cultures to arise in Mesoamerica and perhaps one of the most significant of all the ancient civilizations.

Printed in Poland
by Amazon Fulfillment
Poland Sp. z o.o., Wrocław